D0647036

National Museum of Natural History

BLAKE EDGAR | ILLUSTRATIONS BY JULIUS CSOTONYI

SMITHSONIAN
DINOSAURS
and Other AMAZING CREATURES from DEEP TIME

Smithsonian Books
WASHINGTON, DC

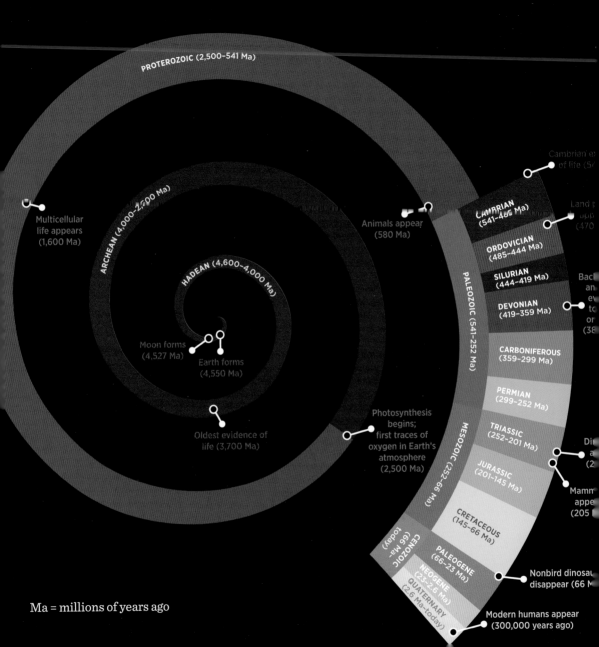

PROTEROZOIC (2,500–541 Ma)

ARCHEAN (4,000–2,500 Ma)

HADEAN (4,600–4,000 Ma)

Multicellular
life appears
(1,600 Ma)

Animals appear
(580 Ma)

Moon forms
(4,527 Ma)

Earth forms
(4,550 Ma)

Oldest evidence of
life (3,700 Ma)

Photosynthesis
begins;
first traces of
oxygen in Earth's
atmosphere
(2,500 Ma)

Cambrian e[x]
of life (5[4]

Land p[lants]
app[ear]
(470[Ma]

CAMBRIAN
(541–485 Ma)

ORDOVICIAN
(485–444 Ma)

SILURIAN
(444–419 Ma)

DEVONIAN
(419–359 Ma)

CARBONIFEROUS
(359–299 Ma)

PERMIAN
(299–252 Ma)

TRIASSIC
(252–201 Ma)

JURASSIC
(201–145 Ma)

CRETACEOUS
(145–66 Ma)

PALEOZOIC (541–252 Ma)

MESOZOIC (252–66 Ma)

CENOZOIC
(66 Ma–
today)

PALEOGENE
(66–23 Ma)

NEOGENE
(23–2.6 Ma)

QUATERNARY
(2.6 Ma–today)

Bac[k]
an[d]
ev[olve]
to[
or[
(38[

Di[nosaurs]
a[ppear]
(2[

Mamm[als]
appe[ar]
(205 [Ma]

Nonbird dinosa[urs]
disappear (66 M[a])

Modern humans appear
(300,000 years ago)

Ma = millions of years ago

Our Planet's Epic Story

Everyone likes a good story, and no story is grander than the saga of Earth and the life on it. It's a very long tale—spanning over 4.5 billion years—but it features plenty of plot twists, scene changes, and a cast of amazing characters. Including you: your body contains traces of life's long journey across deep time, the billions of years from Earth's formation to today.

Earth always has been a dynamic place; as it changes, so does life. Earth's distant past shapes the present in which you play a part, and it influences how the future will unfold. The planet today is a product of enduring geological forces, biological evolution, and climatic change over time. All these factors—plus our actions—will affect the world of tomorrow.

The David H. Koch Hall of Fossils—Deep Time at the Smithsonian National Museum of Natural History is a place where you can explore the grandeur of Earth's history, discover the fossils that reveal the mysteries of life's past 3.7 billion years, ponder how the present world came to be, and prepare for a sustainable future. You'll glimpse ancient life's beauty and diversity in the sea and on land. Following in the footsteps of paleobiologists— scientists who study fossil plants and animals—you'll investigate what can be learned from the rock record of our planet's rich past.

This book takes you from the earliest Earth, just after the planet formed, through successive eras in time and turning points of evolution, up to the age of humans. From the viewpoint of deep time, climates and ecosystems constantly shift, and species come and go. Some groups, like the dinosaurs featured here, endure for vast stretches of time. Our species is still young, yet it is having a huge global impact that will influence the outcome of Earth's next chapter.

From So Simple a Beginning

The early Earth was very different from today's world: in fact, it was a hot and hellish place. Forming about 4.6 billion years ago, the molten planet cooled fairly quickly. By about 2.5 billion years ago, at the end of the Archaen Eon, bacteria were turning carbon dioxide into simple sugars using energy from sunlight. This process—photosynthesis—released oxygen. Over a billion or more years, oxygen grew more abundant, and microbial life grew more complex. But it took longer still for life to get big enough that—had you been around—you'd have been able to spot it without a microscope.

▶ Radioactive elements in zircon minerals, like those in this specimen, can serve as "rock clocks"—they reveal how long ago the rock formed. Scientists can use such dates to figure out the age of fossils found in the rocks, and even when certain events on Earth occurred.

◀ These ribbonlike strands of *Grypania* may represent Earth's oldest-known fossils of eukaryotes (organisms with complex cells that each enclose a nucleus). These are photo-synthetic algae more than 2 billion years old.

▶ Mats of aquatic microbes living in shallow water around a billion years ago trapped sediment in thin layers, eventually forming mound-shaped fossils called stromatolites, like this *Conophyton*.

Animals Arise and Diversity Thrives

After 2 billion years of microbes, evolution produced a sudden, dazzling diversity of complex life. Mysterious beings started to appear 635 million years ago. The soft bodies of these first large multicellular animals left intriguing impressions on muddy seafloors—and left us with many questions, since these Ediacaran animals all went extinct. Later, about 541 million years ago, life really blossomed again during

▲ Shells sheltered Cambrian sea snails such as *Sinuopea eminensis*.

▲ *Pikaia gracilens* had a distinct head and a flexible nerve cord running through its body. These traits made this Burgess Shale fossil a likely precursor to backboned animals.

▲ Trilobites—distinctive hard-shelled arthropods like *Mesonacis vermontanus*—evolved in the Cambrian, the start of their long existence on Earth as marine scavengers and predators.

the Cambrian Period (some Cambrian sea creatures are seen in this painting). Complex animals rapidly evolved and occupied marine realms. As animals began eating one another, they developed shells and other protective hard parts. This burst of biodiversity spawned most major animal groups alive today—including the ancestor of all vertebrates, or animals with backbones, a group that includes human beings.

Life Abounds in Shallow Seas

he next big burst of biodiversity occurred in the warm, shallow seas that covered continents during the Ordovician Period, when the number of marine species tripled within 25 million years. Life swam and burrowed into the seafloor, and the planet's first reefs formed from low-growing corals that provided habitats for bryozoans, crinoids, sponges,

▲ Also called sea lilies, crinoids like *Iocrinus subcrassus* aren't plants but relatives of sea stars. They captured plankton with feathery arms. They were the most abundant, diverse echinoderms of the Ordovician, but most kinds disappeared 252 million years ago.

▼ The first fish had bony shields, like *Dartmuthia gemmifera*, but no jaws. They sucked up particles from the seafloor. Today's jawless lampreys and hagfish still represent their distant relatives.

▲ Corals like *Favistella alveolata* helped form the first reefs, supporting thriving marine invertebrate communities.

▲ During their history—twice as long as that of the dinosaurs—trilobites displayed diverse anatomy and behaviors. *Bumastus decemsegmentus* curled up like a pillbug for protection from predators.

nollusks, and jawless fish. Among the earliest arthropods—the group that includes nsects and spiders—trilobites thrived nd peaked, developing an array of sizes, pines, and complex eyes. Trilobites' time on Earth spanned about 300 million years and spawned more than 15,000 species. The planet's first mass extinction, which was triggered by an ice age 448 million years ago, extinguished many marine species.

Fishes Flourish, and Some Go Ashore

I n a vast ocean rife with reefs, Devonian Period fishes developed jaws for catching or crushing prey such as ammonoids. On land, the first plants, lacking leaves, roots, flowers, and seeds, had already appeared in the Ordovician. Now, early trees, like *Archaeopteris*, spread by spores and grew tall in moist places. The fishlike ancestors of tetrapods (four-footed backboned animals) evolved their legs and feet while still living in the water. These pioneers later would give rise to all land-dwelling vertebrates. As microbes and plants provided food and created habitats, more animals started to come ashore—gradually adapting to a life with sun, air, and gravity.

▲ Armored fish called placoderms, some with lethal, bladelike jaws, dominated Devonian seas. *Bothriolepis canadensis* was quite abundant, but it and all the other placoderms mysteriously went extinct.

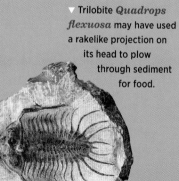

▲ Aquatic amphibian *Acanthostega gunnari* had six-digit hands and feet that it used to paddle or come ashore. One of the oldest tetrapods, *Acanthostega* is a key link in a sequence of fossils that shows the transition from fin to limb.

▼ Trilobite *Quadrops flexuosa* may have used a rakelike projection on its head to plow through sediment for food.

▲ *Archaeopteris*, one of the earliest trees, had a woody trunk and fernlike leaves.

11

The Bug-Filled Swamps of Deep Time

By 320 million years ago, the planet was warm at the equator and cold at the poles. As ice sheets spread out from the South Pole, humid swamps expanded along equatorial coasts, occupied by soaring lycopsid trees, giant tree ferns, and horsetails. Some of the first seed plants (the most common kind of plant today) inhabited drier environments. In this mural, the forest grows in the kind of peaty swamp that formed coal deposits, which humans have mined for fuel. Insects first appeared and took flight in the earlier Devonian Period, but in the Carboniferous, boosted by higher oxygen levels, they developed new forms—and huge sizes. Though smaller now, insects and other arthropods still dominate land ecosystems, composing nine-tenths of all living animals.

▲ *Lepidodendron* and other polelike lycopsid trees covered vast tropical tracts. They could grow more than 100 feet tall without branching, then sprout a crown with spore-filled cones, reproducing just once before dying. The trunks were covered with scalelike leaf bases.

▼ Large ferns distantly related to *Pecopteris arborescens* still grow in tropical forests today.

▲ A less common resident of Carboniferous swamps, tree-sized horsetails like *Annularia spinulosa* grew up to 50 feet tall. Horsetails still grow in wet habitats today but are much shorter.

Lots was happening on land in the Carboniferous Period, but in the sea, it was the golden age of sharks and their kin. More types of these fearsome fishes existed than at any other time in Earth's history. They might have had few competitors for food and few predators (placoderms went extinct about 345 million years ago). Like today's sharks and their relatives, Carboniferous species had skeletons made of cartilage, but they showed notable differences. Some sported a weird whorl of teeth at the front of the jaw. Others had odd-shaped heads and long snouts. Sharks like those in today's oceans didn't arise until much later, during the Cretaceous Period.

◀ Peaking during the Permian Period, the whorl-toothed "shark" *Helicoprion*, actually a ratfish relative, had a bizarre buzz-saw blade of teeth whose fit and function have puzzled paleontologists.

▲ The strange, anvil-shaped brush of calcified cartilage behind the head of *Akmonistion zangerli* (from today's Scotland) may have identified this fish to others of its species. This shark is seen at the bottom of the illustration opposite.

▼ Odd-looking shark relative *Edestus heinrichsii* had curved jaws full of sharp teeth. You can see it hunting in the painting at left.

Here Comes the Sun

Without the sun and plants, we wouldn't exist. Plants laid the foundation for a web of life by transforming carbon dioxide from the air into simple sugars and other substances that animals could eat, and by generating oxygen. The first modern ecosystems—in which back-boned animals gain energy by eating plants—emerged during the Permian Period. By this time, Earth's land masses had assembled into a single supercontinent called Pangaea. Ferns, lycopsids, and seed plants such as cycads, ginkgoes, and conifers covered the ground. As the climate got drier during the Permian, seed plants became more common. This botanical boom opened opportunities for plant-eating animals, or herbivores, setting the stage for a major transition in Earth's terrestrial (land) environments.

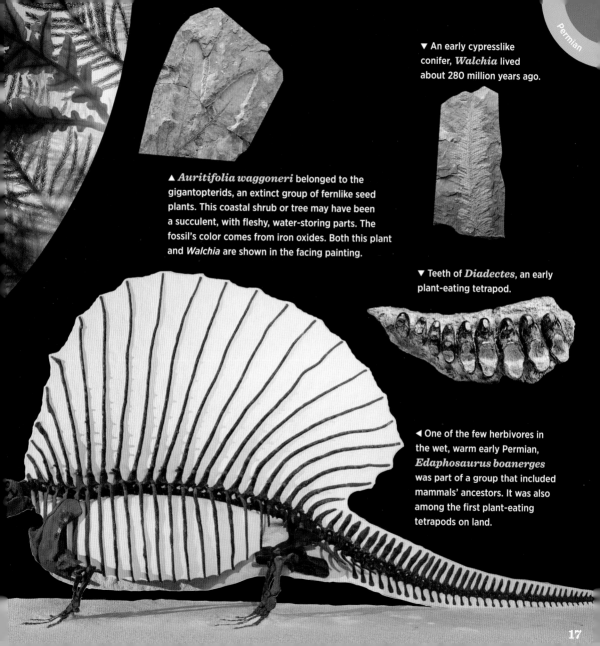

▼ An early cypresslike conifer, *Walchia* lived about 280 million years ago.

▲ *Auritifolia waggoneri* belonged to the gigantopterids, an extinct group of fernlike seed plants. This coastal shrub or tree may have been a succulent, with fleshy, water-storing parts. The fossil's color comes from iron oxides. Both this plant and *Walchia* are shown in the facing painting.

▼ Teeth of *Diadectes*, an early plant-eating tetrapod.

◄ One of the few herbivores in the wet, warm early Permian, *Edaphosaurus boanerges* was part of a group that included mammals' ancestors. It was also among the first plant-eating tetrapods on land.

Snapping Synapsids Steal the Scene

Although plants were plentiful in the early Permian, around 290 million years ago, few big herbivores had evolved yet. Insects and other arthropods devoured living and dead plants. Tiny animals also ate rotting matter and debris, returning nutrients to the soil. Otherwise, Earth remained largely a carnivore-eat-carnivore world. Synapsids composed a common and diverse group of carnivores and herbivores. Although synapsids are sometimes called "mammal-like reptiles," and *Dimetrodon* (in background below) is sometimes called a dinosaur, all synapsids actually were close mammal relatives. Large, swamp-dwelling amphibians, including *Eryops*, were also an important part of the Permian world.

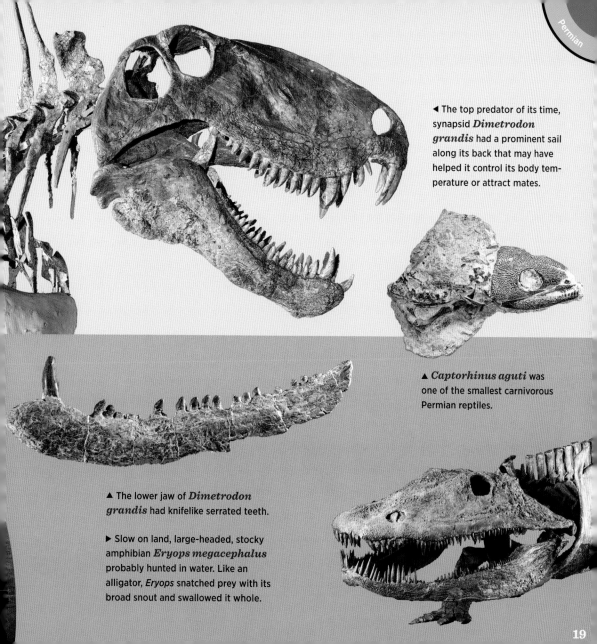

◀ The top predator of its time, synapsid *Dimetrodon grandis* had a prominent sail along its back that may have helped it control its body temperature or attract mates.

▲ *Captorhinus aguti* was one of the smallest carnivorous Permian reptiles.

▲ The lower jaw of *Dimetrodon grandis* had knifelike serrated teeth.

▶ Slow on land, large-headed, stocky amphibian *Eryops megacephalus* probably hunted in water. Like an alligator, *Eryops* snatched prey with its broad snout and swallowed it whole.

Make Room for Plant Eaters

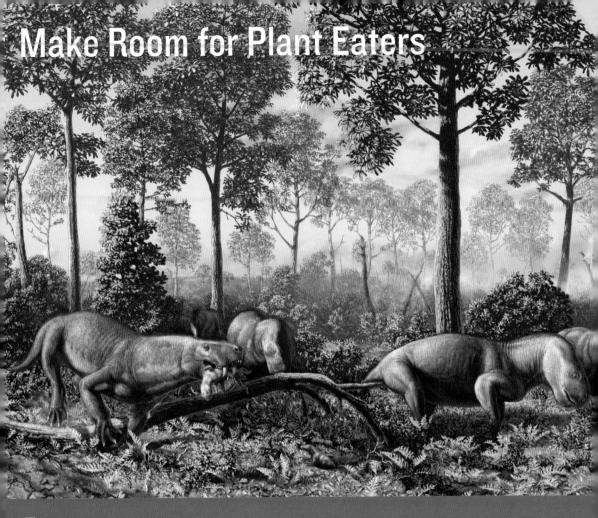

Large herbivores, or plant eaters, evolved and eventually outnumbered carnivores during the Permian—setting up an ecological balance that continues today. It took time for herbivores to show up in large numbers, though, because they first had to evolve the ability to digest plants' cellulose. Successful plant eaters, such as the dicynodont lineage of synapsids, had to develop sharp beaks and huge jaw muscles to slice plants into pieces.

▲ *Platypodosaurus robustus* had a pair of downward-pointing tusks alongside its plant-shredding beak. This dicynodont comes from a region of South Africa renowned for synapsid fossils.

▲ Sturdy legs helped reptile relative *Seymouria baylorensis* move easily on land, but it reproduced in water. It didn't have the kind of eggs—amniotic ones, which hold an embryo in a sac of fluid—that let reptiles, birds, and mammals live full-time on land.

▶ First described in 1860 by Richard Owen, the paleontologist who came up with the term Dinosauria (the formal name for dinosaurs), *Oudenodon bainii* was another plant-eating South African dicynodont.

Most dicynodonts lacked teeth. Ranging in size from rat to elephant, dicynodonts evolved in the Middle Permian, and some of them survived until late in the following Triassic Period.

Worst Extinction Ever

arth has experienced five great mass extinctions—events when more than half of living species died out within a million years. The end-Permian extinction, 252 million years ago, was by far the biggest to date. Massive volcanic eruptions in Siberia spewed lava over 2.7 million square miles and triggered rapid climate change as greenhouse gases escaped from burning coal deposits. Acid rain altered ocean chemistry and killed

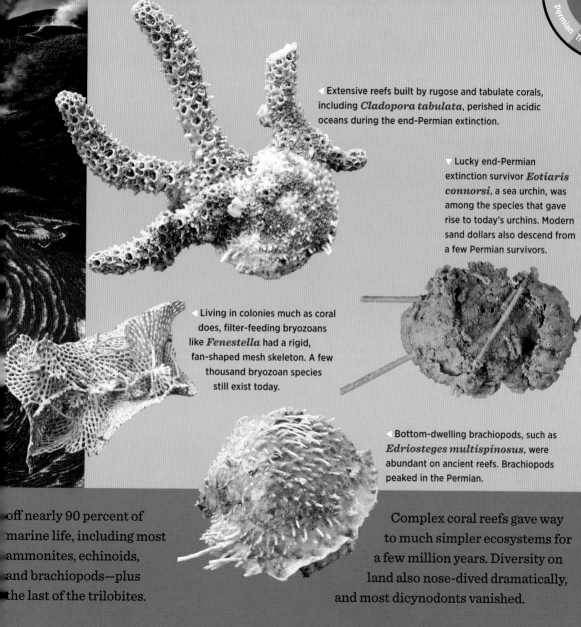

Extensive reefs built by rugose and tabulate corals, including *Cladopora tabulata*, perished in acidic oceans during the end-Permian extinction.

Lucky end-Permian extinction survivor *Eotiaris connorsi*, a sea urchin, was among the species that gave rise to today's urchins. Modern sand dollars also descend from a few Permian survivors.

Living in colonies much as coral does, filter-feeding bryozoans like *Fenestella* had a rigid, fan-shaped mesh skeleton. A few thousand bryozoan species still exist today.

Bottom-dwelling brachiopods, such as *Edriosteges multispinosus*, were abundant on ancient reefs. Brachiopods peaked in the Permian.

off nearly 90 percent of marine life, including most ammonites, echinoids, and brachiopods—plus the last of the trilobites.

Complex coral reefs gave way to much simpler ecosystems for a few million years. Diversity on land also nose-dived dramatically, and most dicynodonts vanished.

Dawn of the Dinosaurs

Life rebounded in a riot of evolution during the Triassic Period. Perhaps no time since the Cambrian had seen such swift shifts in animal diversity, including the first appearance of frogs, turtles, and mammals, plus flying pterosaurs and land-dwelling dinosaurs. Nearly all main groups of living terrestrial tetrapods evolved in this period. Reptiles—minor players in the Permian—now were the most numerous kinds of new large animals, and they lived on land and in the water and sky, rapidly diversifying into new habitats and roles in a Triassic world without polar ice caps, where most places were hot and dry or warm and wet. By the Late Triassic, dinosaurs were still a reptilian minority, but some had already grown quite big.

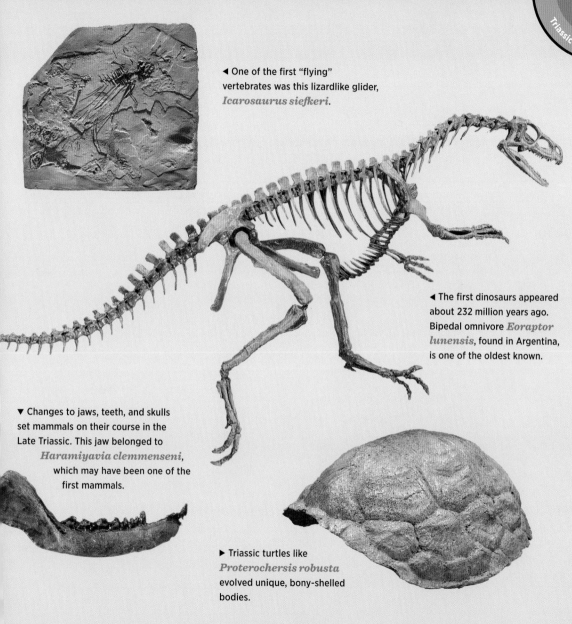

◀ One of the first "flying" vertebrates was this lizardlike glider, *Icarosaurus siefkeri*.

◀ The first dinosaurs appeared about 232 million years ago. Bipedal omnivore *Eoraptor lunensis*, found in Argentina, is one of the oldest known.

▼ Changes to jaws, teeth, and skulls set mammals on their course in the Late Triassic. This jaw belonged to *Haramiyavia clemmenseni*, which may have been one of the first mammals.

▶ Triassic turtles like *Proterochersis robusta* evolved unique, bony-shelled bodies.

Reptiles of the Sea

Early in the Triassic, many reptiles returned to the sea to join—and eat—the bony fishes and abundant mollusks there. Placodonts, like the pair at left, paddling in pursuit of bivalves, could crush clams, snails, and brachiopods with their broad, flat teeth. More streamlined, web-footed nothosaurs and thalattosaurs (like *Askeptosaurus* shown above) snagged fishes with the aid of long snouts and sharp teeth. The first teleosts (bony fishes with a symmetrical tail fin and extendible jaws) evolved in the Triassic around 215 million years ago; today, almost all fish species belong to this group.

▶ The skull of placodont ("plate tooth") *Macroplacus raeticus* had strong jaws to help this reptile's flat teeth crush shellfish.

▼ Slender-bodied *Askeptosaurus italicus* was a primitive member of the thalattosaurs, a group of marine reptiles that lived only during the Triassic.

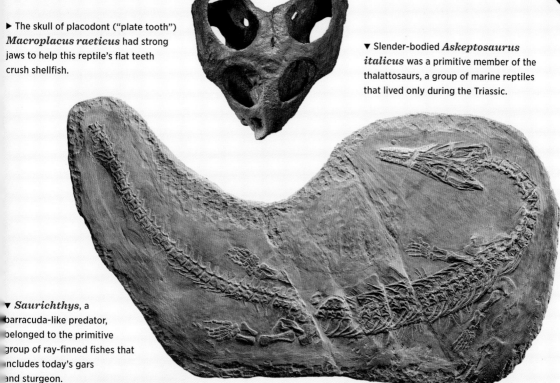

▼ *Saurichthys*, a barracuda-like predator, belonged to the primitive group of ray-finned fishes that includes today's gars and sturgeon.

▶ Nothosaur *Neusticosaurus edwardsii* swam by undulating its long body and tail.

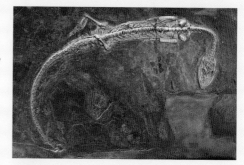

27

Jurassic Giants

As the supercontinent Pangaea split apart, more volcanic eruptions—and another mass extinction—marked the end of the Triassic. These events, while bad news for many animals, proved an advantage for dinosaurs, a group of creatures that are classified together because of similarities in their arm, hand, and hip anatomy. In the Jurassic Period, their time really arrived.

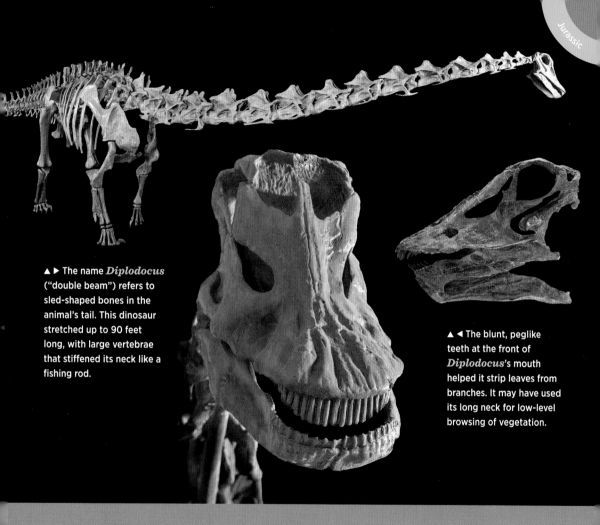

▲ ▶ The name *Diplodocus* ("double beam") refers to sled-shaped bones in the animal's tail. This dinosaur stretched up to 90 feet long, with large vertebrae that stiffened its neck like a fishing rod.

▲ ◀ The blunt, peglike teeth at the front of *Diplodocus*'s mouth helped it strip leaves from branches. It may have used its long neck for low-level browsing of vegetation.

Dinosaurs became very abundant and diverse—and much bigger. They lived from pole to pole and along emerging inland seas. Sauropods, the largest dinosaurs (or any other sort of animal) ever to walk on Earth, far surpassed the size of even the biggest land mammals. Being huge helped protect them from predators but also meant they needed more energy to grow and move, so they devoured enormous amounts of plants.

Variations on a Very Large Theme

Two of the most common sauropods found in the rock layers of the Morrison Formation, which extends across the American West, *Diplodocus* and *Camarasaurus* demonstrate the different directions taken by these immense creatures. On the smaller side for a sauropod, *Camarasaurus lentus* (whose fossils are shown here) had a long neck that let it reach treetops or drop down to the ground. Microwear on the two species' teeth suggests that stocky *Camarasaurus* ate coarser vegetation than *Diplodocus* did. Sauropods had similar strategies for sustaining their huge size: their vertebrae had hollow spaces filled with air sacs, which lightened the load on their bones without sacrificing strength. A powerful heart (and possibly high blood pressure) sent blood up to the brain. Thick limb bones supported their bulky bodies, which contained huge guts to digest plants.

Camarasaurus lentus cropped leaves and other vegetation with broad, spoon-shaped teeth. Paleontologists have found numerous skulls from this species.

Top Theropod of Its Time

Giant sauropods were closely related to predatory carnivorous dinosaurs called theropods. In the Jurassic, around 150 million years ago, one of the largest theropods was *Allosaurus*, reaching 30 feet long and weighing at least a ton. *Allosaurus* had large hands and claws and a lightweight skull. All dinosaurs laid shelled eggs of various shapes—both spherical and ovoid—and the biggest might have topped 10 inches long. Many dinosaurs probably incubated their eggs in nests of dirt and vegetation on the ground, as modern crocodilians and some birds do today. In this mural, crocodile relative *Macelognathus* raids an *Allosaurus* nest to capture a hatchling.

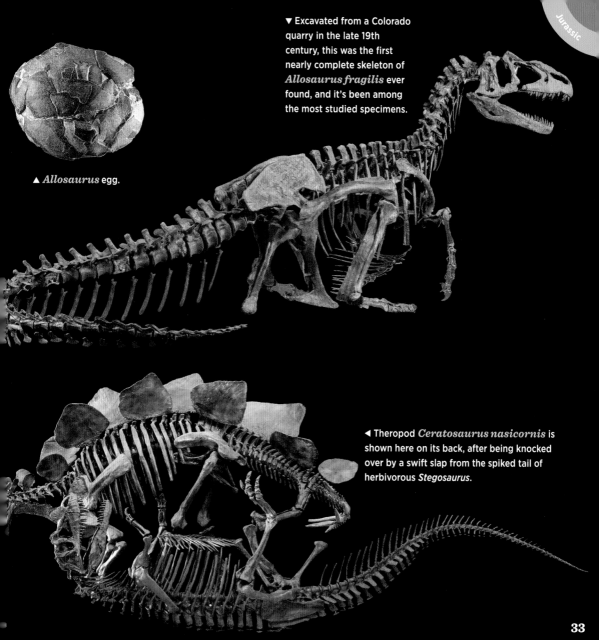

▼ Excavated from a Colorado quarry in the late 19th century, this was the first nearly complete skeleton of *Allosaurus fragilis* ever found, and it's been among the most studied specimens.

▲ *Allosaurus* egg.

◄ Theropod *Ceratosaurus nasicornis* is shown here on its back, after being knocked over by a swift slap from the spiked tail of herbivorous *Stegosaurus*.

Grow Fast or Die Young

Dinosaurs began life out of the nest as small, vulnerable hatchlings. Within 20 years, most reached their adult size, whether that was as small as a turkey or as big as a bus. They had growth spurts, much like human teenagers do, and they got big quickly (compare the sizes of adult and juvenile specimens of the ornithopod dinosaur *Camptosaurus dispar*). Counting the annual growth rings in fossil bone reveals just how rapidly dinosaurs grew up. Getting big fast gave dinosaurs a chance against predators, and maybe it also gave baby dinosaurs an edge in "outgrowing" competition for food with other animals, even mammals. Many Jurassic ecosystems contained more species of mammals than dinosaurs.

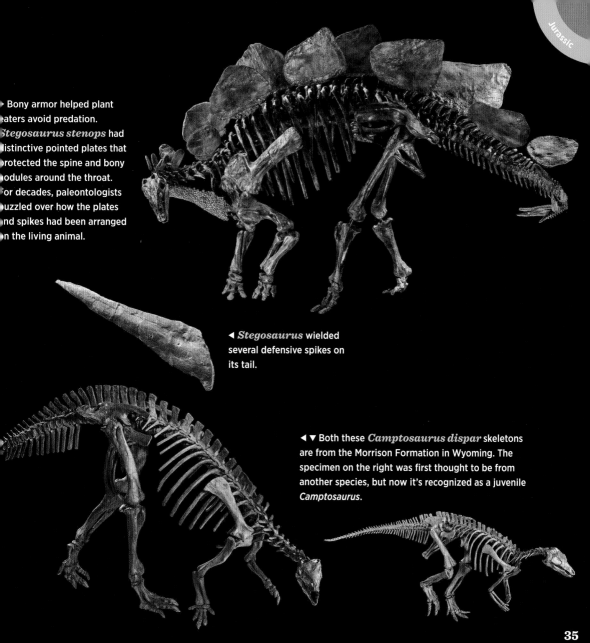

Bony armor helped plant eaters avoid predation. *Stegosaurus stenops* had distinctive pointed plates that protected the spine and bony nodules around the throat. For decades, paleontologists puzzled over how the plates and spikes had been arranged in the living animal.

◄ *Stegosaurus* wielded several defensive spikes on its tail.

◄ ▼ Both these *Camptosaurus dispar* skeletons are from the Morrison Formation in Wyoming. The specimen on the right was first thought to be from another species, but now it's recognized as a juvenile *Camptosaurus*.

35

Mollusks on the Move

Despite marine invertebrate extinctions at the turn of the Triassic and still more turmoil in the Jurassic, mollusks and other groups had recovered and diversified by the Middle Jurassic. Many modern marine invertebrates—including scallops, oysters, and other bivalves that burrowed into the seabed—evolved at this time. Although they'd faced near-elimination in the end-Permian mass extinction, crinoids,

▲ Squidlike *Acanthoteuthis speciosa* sported an ink sac and 10 tentacles with tiny hooks. Its relatives, the belemnites, had bullet-shaped shell ends that are now commonly found as fossils.

◄ Horseshoe crabs—little changed since their first appearance in the fossil record—still have shield-shaped carapaces. This Jurassic species is *Mesolimulus walchi*.

◄ Whether large or small, like those of *Promicroceras planicosta*, ammonite shells contained gas-filled chambers for flotation.

▲ A well-preserved prawn, *Aeger armatus*, lies in limestone formed in an ancient lagoon.

ea urchins, sea stars, and other echino-lerms now proliferated. Further evolution-ry "experimentation" occurred among rustaceans and cephalopods. This mural shows a floating community of crimson crinoids suspended from a log covered with bivalves, surrounded by darting squid and ammonites.

Much More besides Dinosaurs

Like the dinosaurs, other groups of reptiles from the Triassic thrived on into the Jurassic. Sea-dwelling predators evolved flippers and fins (but still had to return to the surface to breathe). The strong, vertical tail fin of ichthyosaurs propelled them through the water like tuna, and they steered with pectoral flippers. Plesiosaurs (like *Rhomaleosaurus*, chasing *Pachycormus* above) used their four large, winglike flippers to swim like sea turtles. Both ichthyosaurs and plesiosaurs gave birth to live young. Pterosaurs, meanwhile, became the first active flyers, evolving some 80 million years before the first birds took flight.

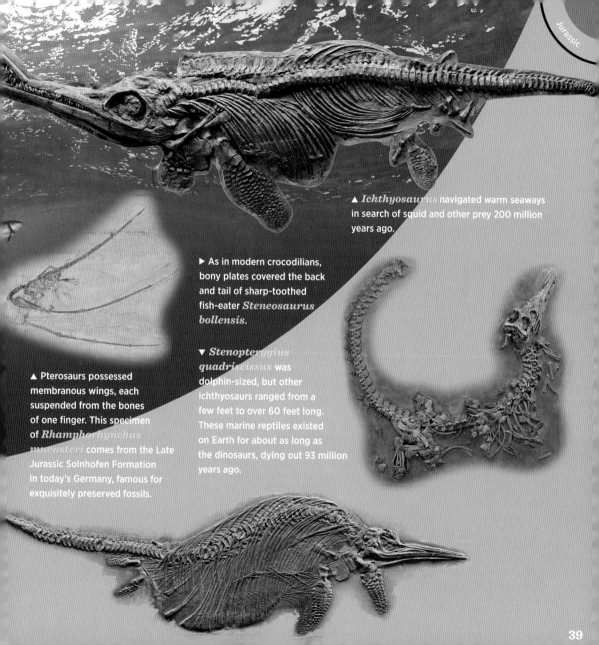

▲ *Ichthyosaurus* navigated warm seaways in search of squid and other prey 200 million years ago.

▶ As in modern crocodilians, bony plates covered the back and tail of sharp-toothed fish-eater *Steneosaurus bollensis*.

▼ *Stenopterygius quadriscissus* was dolphin-sized, but other ichthyosaurs ranged from a few feet to over 60 feet long. These marine reptiles existed on Earth for about as long as the dinosaurs, dying out 93 million years ago.

▲ Pterosaurs possessed membranous wings, each suspended from the bones of one finger. This specimen of *Rhamphorhynchus muensteri* comes from the Late Jurassic Solnhofen Formation in today's Germany, famous for exquisitely preserved fossils.

Paleontologists have traced birds' origins back to a group of small, nonflying theropod dinosaurs known as maniraptorans. The first feathered dinosaurs didn't fly; their feathers were just for body insulation or possibly for display. The earliest known flying bird is *Archaeopteryx*, and birds evolved into a wide range of sizes and shapes by the time of the end-Cretaceous mass extinction, which eliminated the rest of the dinosaurs. Fortunately, some bird groups survived—and they're the source of all living bird species. Since there are now thousands more species of birds than there are of mammals, you could say that dinosaurs *still* dominate Earth today. (This mural shows the bird *Avisaurus* perched above the dinosaur *Troodon*.)

Birds Are Dinosaurs

▶ One of a dozen examples of the oldest known flying bird, the "Berlin specimen" of *Archaeopteryx lithographica* displays well-developed wing feathers, with which the toothed bird flew 155 million years ago.

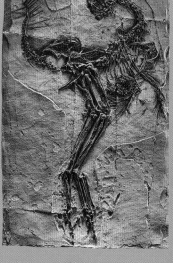

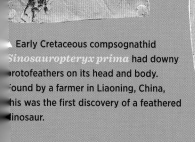

▲ Early Cretaceous compsognathid *Sinosauropteryx prima* had downy protofeathers on its head and body. Found by a farmer in Liaoning, China, this was the first discovery of a feathered dinosaur.

▼ Among the earliest birds with a toothless beak, *Confuciusornis dui* links *Archaeopteryx* to more modern birds.

▲ The maniraptoran *Caudipteryx zoui* was among the first dinosaurs to have well-developed feathers, including a tail plume.

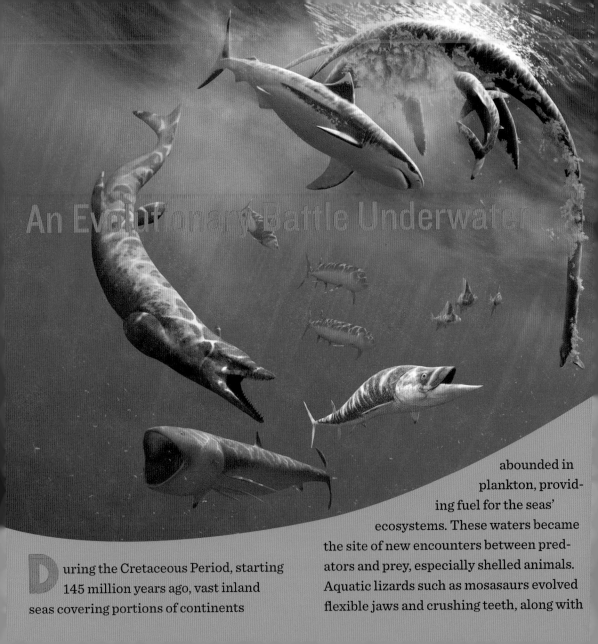

An Evolutionary Battle Underwater

During the Cretaceous Period, starting 145 million years ago, vast inland seas covering portions of continents abounded in plankton, providing fuel for the seas' ecosystems. These waters became the site of new encounters between predators and prey, especially shelled animals. Aquatic lizards such as mosasaurs evolved flexible jaws and crushing teeth, along with

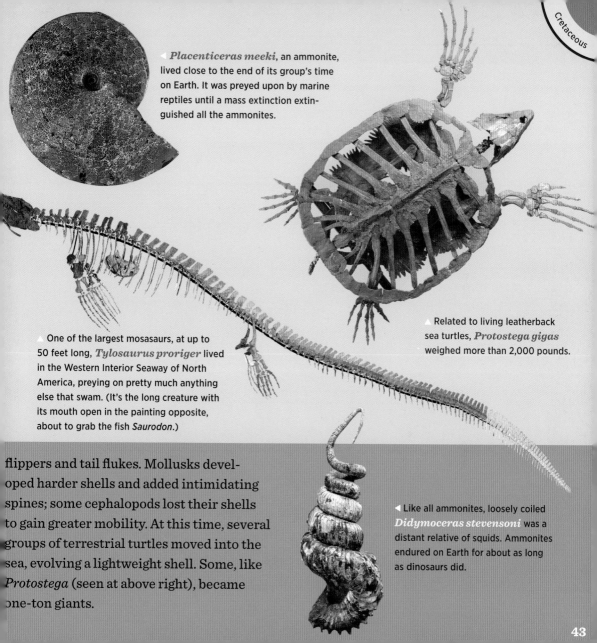

Placenticeras meeki, an ammonite, lived close to the end of its group's time on Earth. It was preyed upon by marine reptiles until a mass extinction extinguished all the ammonites.

Related to living leatherback sea turtles, *Protostega gigas* weighed more than 2,000 pounds.

One of the largest mosasaurs, at up to 50 feet long, *Tylosaurus proriger* lived in the Western Interior Seaway of North America, preying on pretty much anything else that swam. (It's the long creature with its mouth open in the painting opposite, about to grab the fish *Saurodon*.)

flippers and tail flukes. Mollusks developed harder shells and added intimidating spines; some cephalopods lost their shells to gain greater mobility. At this time, several groups of terrestrial turtles moved into the sea, evolving a lightweight shell. Some, like *Protostega* (seen at above right), became one-ton giants.

Like all ammonites, loosely coiled *Didymoceras stevensoni* was a distant relative of squids. Ammonites endured on Earth for about as long as dinosaurs did.

A Fishy Final Meal

O cean food webs tend to harbor more predators of different sizes than those on land, and in Late Cretaceous seas, carnivorous fishes were the most abundant hunters. In this mural, a pair of the enormous teleost fish *Xiphactinus audax* cruise along—one caught in the act of swallowing *Hesperornis*, the diving bird also shown in the foreground. A similar act of predation has been frozen in time as a fossil

One fish, two fish: *Thryptodus zitteli* was swallowed headfirst by the much larger *Xiphactinus audax*.

Nearly wingless bird *Hesperornis regalis* lived in the Late Cretaceous and preyed on fishes. It somewhat resembled a modern cormorant, but its beak contained a set of sharp teeth.

The skull of bony-tongued *Pachyrhizodus*, a fish related to today's tarpon.

seen at the top of this page: as its last meal, our *Xiphactinus* swallowed the whole body of another teleost, *Thryptodus zitteli*. Being a fish—or even a bird—in these waters was isky business.

About 75 million years ago, in the Late Cretaceous, dinosaurs were abundant and more diverse than ever. Their warm world had widespread forest ecosystems. Although the continents were moving close to their present geographic positions, a seaway stretching from the Arctic Ocean to the Caribbean Sea divided North America. Sauropods were now limited to the titanosaurs, but other dinosaur groups—such as ankylosaurs, tyrannosaurs, and ceratopsians—evolved many new species. Curious anatomical features appeared from head to toe (or tail) on these new creatures, including thick-domed skulls, elaborate bony frills, and tail clubs. This mural shows two ankylosaurs browsing near an advancing *Gorgosaurus* at left.

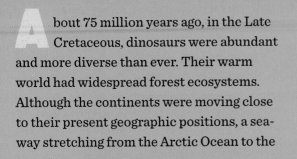

Dinosaurs Hit Their Peak

▲ Tanklike ankylosaur *Euoplocephalus tutus* had knobby bones called osteoderms embedded in the skin of its back and a tail club formed of fused osteoderms. This wide-mouthed browser had a large gut for processing plants.

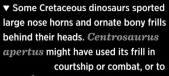

▶ *Gorgosaurus libratus* was a primitive member of the two-fingered, meat-eating theropods called tyrannosaurs.

▼ Some Cretaceous dinosaurs sported large nose horns and ornate bony frills behind their heads. *Centrosaurus apertus* might have used its frill in courtship or combat, or to signal to others of its kind.

▲ The bizarre skull of pachycephalosaur *Stegoceras validum* bore many knobs and spikes around a dome of bone several inches thick—useful features, as these dinosaurs may have butted each other in dominance displays.

Dinosaurs in a Flowering World

Relative newcomers in Earth history, flowering plants, or angiosperms, first appeared about 130 million years ago in the Early Cretaceous. They reproduced via pollen transported between plants by insects or wind, and sprouted and grew quickly. By the Late Cretaceous, many flowering plants were thriving in a range of habitats, sharing space with conifers, ferns, and increasingly rare cycads. Today, angiosperms account for 90 percent of plant species—including all the grains, fruits, and vegetables we enjoy.

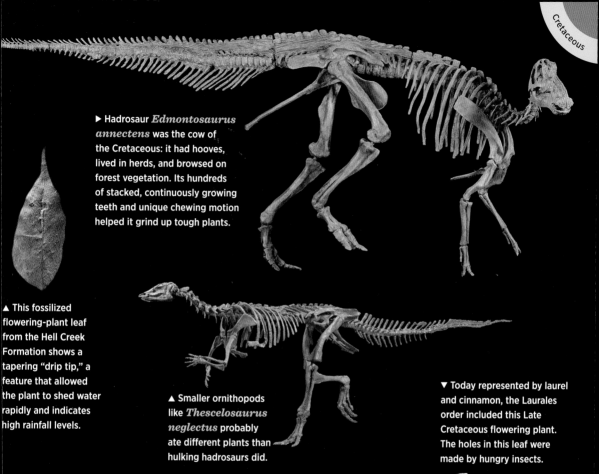

▶ Hadrosaur *Edmontosaurus annectens* was the cow of the Cretaceous: it had hooves, lived in herds, and browsed on forest vegetation. Its hundreds of stacked, continuously growing teeth and unique chewing motion helped it grind up tough plants.

▲ This fossilized flowering-plant leaf from the Hell Creek Formation shows a tapering "drip tip," a feature that allowed the plant to shed water rapidly and indicates high rainfall levels.

▲ Smaller ornithopods like *Thescelosaurus neglectus* probably ate different plants than hulking hadrosaurs did.

▼ Today represented by laurel and cinnamon, the Laurales order included this Late Cretaceous flowering plant. The holes in this leaf were made by hungry insects.

Duck-billed hadrosaurs, like the trio of *Edmontosaurus* shown in this picture, diversified and adapted so they could eat the Late Cretaceous's botanical bounty. The dinosaur and plant fossils shown here date to nearly the end of the dinosaurs' reign.

King of Cretaceous Carnivores

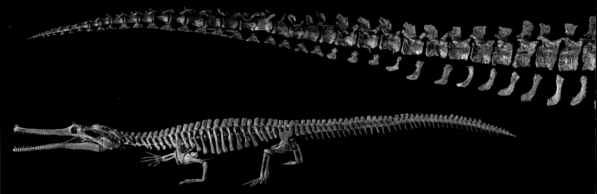

▲ An ancient reptile resembling long-snouted, fish-eating modern crocodilians, *Champsosaurus laramiensis* filled a similar ecological role in its environment. *Champsosaurus* survived for 30 million years after the end-Cretaceous extinction.

▼ Alligator *Stangerochampsa* snagged prey with its front teeth and crushed bones with its rear ones. It died out with the dinosaurs.

n its time, *Tyrannosaurus rex* was the largest meat eater in western North America. It feasted on dinosaurs large and small—including *Triceratops*, as seen here—gulping down flesh and bone in massive bites. It weighed in at more than 15,000 pounds and 42 feet long, so no other carnivore could touch the "king of the tyrant lizards" (as its name means in Latin). This skeleton, found in 1988 by a Montana

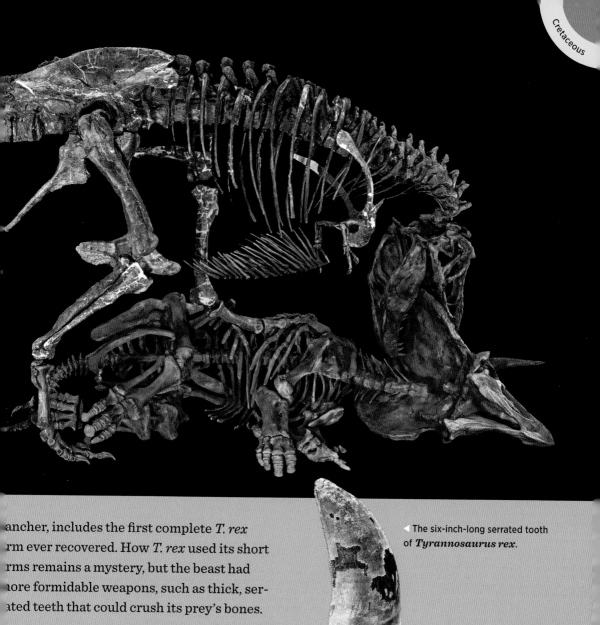

ancher, includes the first complete *T. rex*
rm ever recovered. How *T. rex* used its short
rms remains a mystery, but the beast had
ore formidable weapons, such as thick, ser-
ated teeth that could crush its prey's bones.

◀ The six-inch-long serrated tooth
of *Tyrannosaurus rex*.

Death from Outer Space

Earth's most recent mass extinction happened 66 million years ago when a 6-mile-wide asteroid slammed into the planet. The impact triggered tsunamis, wildfires, earthquakes, and maybe even volcanic eruptions. Vaporized, sulfur-rich rocks from the impact site caused global cooling. Debris and other traces of this cosmic collision have been found around the globe, including a submerged crater near Mexico. Asteroids have hit Earth many times in its long history, but no other is known to have caused so much destruction. Controversial at first, the impact explanation for this extinction has become broadly accepted as scientists added evidence to strengthen their case. Besides dinosaurs, the extinction wiped out three-quarters of Earth's species, including pterosaurs, many lizards, and ammonites, but spared many plants, crocodilians, birds, and mammals.

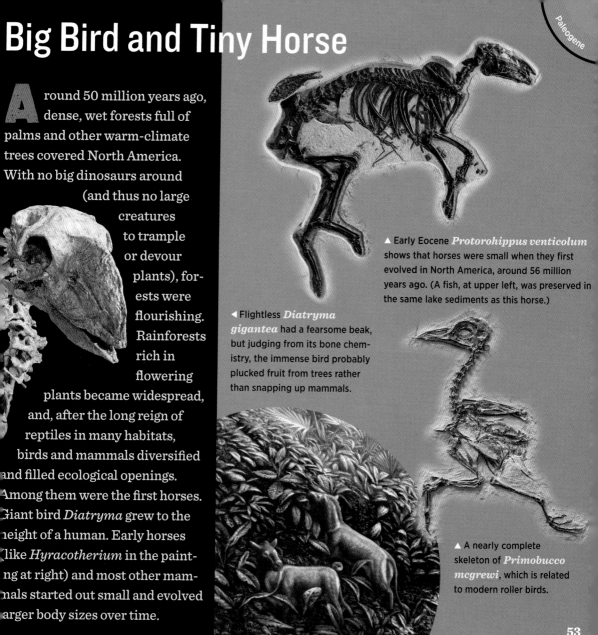

Big Bird and Tiny Horse

Around 50 million years ago, dense, wet forests full of palms and other warm-climate trees covered North America. With no big dinosaurs around (and thus no large creatures to trample or devour plants), forests were flourishing. Rainforests rich in flowering plants became widespread, and, after the long reign of reptiles in many habitats, birds and mammals diversified and filled ecological openings. Among them were the first horses. Giant bird *Diatryma* grew to the height of a human. Early horses (like *Hyracotherium* in the painting at right) and most other mammals started out small and evolved larger body sizes over time.

▲ Early Eocene *Protorohippus venticolum* shows that horses were small when they first evolved in North America, around 56 million years ago. (A fish, at upper left, was preserved in the same lake sediments as this horse.)

◄ Flightless *Diatryma gigantea* had a fearsome beak, but judging from its bone chemistry, the immense bird probably plucked fruit from trees rather than snapping up mammals.

▲ A nearly complete skeleton of *Primobucco mcgrewi*, which is related to modern roller birds.

53

Mammals Take Center Stage

Mammals that survived the Cretaceous-Paleogene mass extinction hit the evolutionary jackpot and rapidly gave rise to most modern mammal groups. In less than 5 million years, an incredible array of mammals evolved bigger bodies and new ways to eat. Fifty-six million years ago, an episode of global warming (which was swift but still much slower than today's) brought drier conditions that changed both mammals and plants. Some mammals evolved smaller bodies. In a later, cooler phase of the Eocene Epoch, open woodlands provided a fast-growing food supply for herds of browsing mammals—which stalking and sprinting carnivores ate. Small browsers chose the most nutritious plants, but big ones instead often ranged widely to find enough to eat.

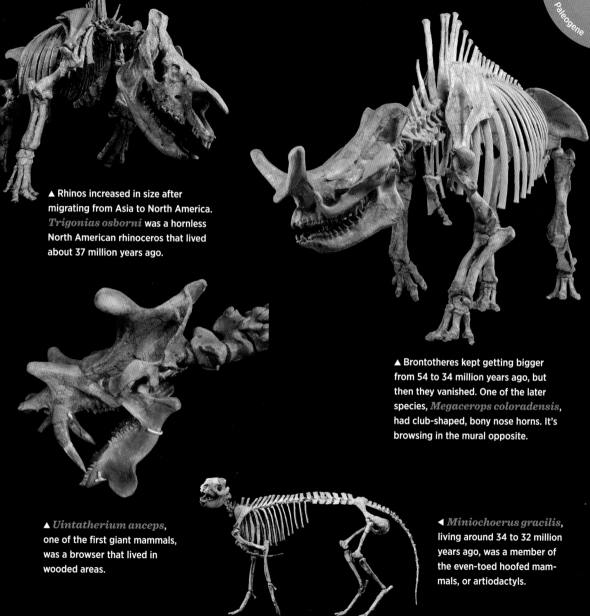

▲ Rhinos increased in size after migrating from Asia to North America. *Trigonias osborni* was a hornless North American rhinoceros that lived about 37 million years ago.

▲ Brontotheres kept getting bigger from 54 to 34 million years ago, but then they vanished. One of the later species, *Megacerops coloradensis*, had club-shaped, bony nose horns. It's browsing in the mural opposite.

▲ *Uintatherium anceps*, one of the first giant mammals, was a browser that lived in wooded areas.

◀ *Miniochoerus gracilis*, living around 34 to 32 million years ago, was a member of the even-toed hoofed mammals, or artiodactyls.

55

Mammals Explore High and Low

Peering down on palms, spiral gingers, and a thirsty *Uintatherium* below, this mural shows how North American mammals moved vertically to take advantage of new Eocene ecological opportunities. The primate *Notharctus* reaches out from a branch to pick ripe laurel fruit, which it spotted with its 3D color vision. Besides grasping hands and forward-facing eyes, distinctive primate traits include very flexible forelimbs and a large brain relative to body size. Ancient bat *Icaronycteris*, among the first of the sole group of mammals that evolved true flight, swerves past in pursuit of insects. Some mammals that couldn't climb or fly took to digging underground, seeking shelter from predators or temperature extremes.

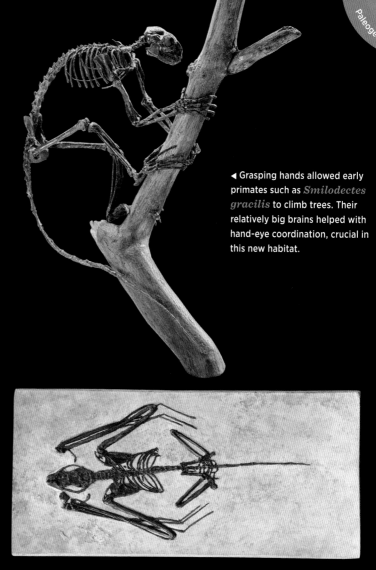

◄ Grasping hands allowed early primates such as *Smilodectes gracilis* to climb trees. Their relatively big brains helped with hand-eye coordination, crucial in this new habitat.

▲ Early bat *Icaronycteris index* ate insects but couldn't echolocate for them in flight. A long tail and lack of leg membrane were among its many primitive traits.

Mammals Become Mariners

Several lineages of marine mammals, from otters to whales, live in the sea today. Oceans offer abundant sources of protein, and, starting 55 million years ago, some mammals began to change many of their organs and body functions to survive there. Moving landmasses and atmospheric changes caused the oceans to cool about 34 million years ago, and currents carried up nutrients from the depths—which became the basis for new marine ecosystems. Phytoplankton and zooplankton flourished and provided a rich food supply. Baleen whales evolved an efficient feeding technique and eventually became Earth's largest animals ever. Distant relatives of elephants, the sirenians, or sea cows, also evolved in the Eocene.

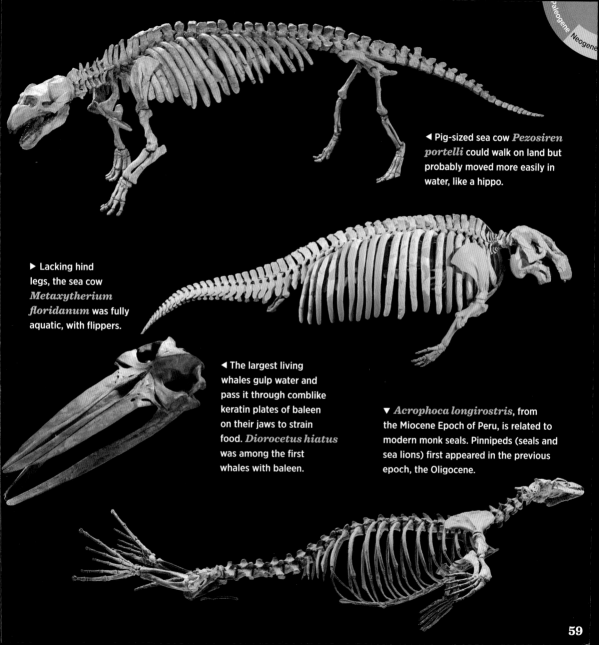

◀ Pig-sized sea cow *Pezosiren portelli* could walk on land but probably moved more easily in water, like a hippo.

▶ Lacking hind legs, the sea cow *Metaxytherium floridanum* was fully aquatic, with flippers.

◀ The largest living whales gulp water and pass it through comblike keratin plates of baleen on their jaws to strain food. *Diorocetus hiatus* was among the first whales with baleen.

▼ *Acrophoca longirostris*, from the Miocene Epoch of Peru, is related to modern monk seals. Pinnipeds (seals and sea lions) first appeared in the previous epoch, the Oligocene.

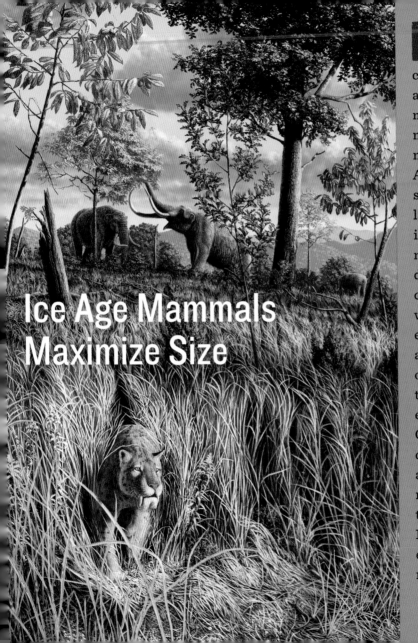

Ice Age Mammals Maximize Size

Bigger bodies do better in cooler climates. The colder it got during the last ice age, the larger many mammals evolved to be. A small number of large mammals, or megafauna, still exist in North America, but dozens more such species roamed here late in the Quaternary Period, including ground sloths, mammoths, mastodons, dire wolves, and sabertooth cats. Ice ages can happen when temperatures drop enough for ice sheets to form and thicken. The most recent one ended 11,700 years ago. By that time, humans had already expanded around the globe. Our species' spread coincided with the rapid decline and disappearance of large mammals—especially from the Americas and Australasia. Hunting and other kinds of ecosystem changes pushed many mammals to extinction.

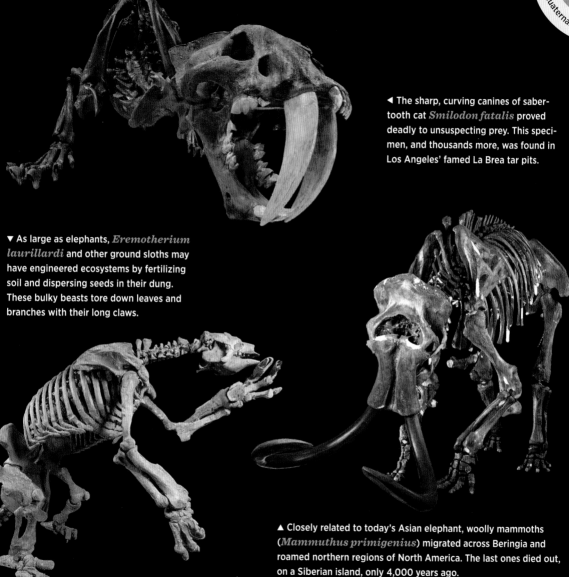

◄ The sharp, curving canines of saber-tooth cat *Smilodon fatalis* proved deadly to unsuspecting prey. This specimen, and thousands more, was found in Los Angeles' famed La Brea tar pits.

▼ As large as elephants, *Eremotherium laurillardi* and other ground sloths may have engineered ecosystems by fertilizing soil and dispersing seeds in their dung. These bulky beasts tore down leaves and branches with their long claws.

▲ Closely related to today's Asian elephant, woolly mammoths (*Mammuthus primigenius*) migrated across Beringia and roamed northern regions of North America. The last ones died out, on a Siberian island, only 4,000 years ago.

The Rise of Humans

Humans have always been curious explorers. We embarked from Africa not long after our species evolved there, at least 300,000 years ago, and we occupied environments worldwide. Human ingenuity led to the development of tools and weapons, which we increasingly used to get food and control nature. We became top predators and a global, fast-paced force of nature. Our impact has been so profound that some suggest a new geological epoch should be named for us: the Anthropocene, or Age of Humans. Our species has also evolved the capacity to learn from the past, plan for our future, debate ideas, and make decisions. We can choose to reduce our impact on the planet, use resources wisely, and improve the fate of other species—and thus avert another mass extinction.

▼ Green sea turtle (*Chelonia mydas*)—whose ancestors evolved in the Cretaceous—is one of seven species of marine turtle under threat of extinction today because of human activity.

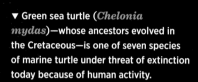

◄ Once only a huge eagle preyed upon the giant flightless moas of New Zealand. After humans arrived, though, *Dinornis robustus* and eight other moa species all perished within a century or two.

◄ Human action can avert extinction. Protection and a pesticide ban let our once-endangered national symbol, the bald eagle (*Haliaeetus leucocephalus*), rebound in increasing numbers. This bird is young, so its head feathers are still dark.

Published on the occasion of the opening of the David H. Koch Hall of Fossils—Deep Time at the Smithsonian National Museum of Natural History

National Museum of Natural History
Director: Kirk R. Johnson
Book development team and scientific review: Anna K. Behrensmeyer, Matthew T. Carrano, Ashley Jenson, Kirk R. Johnson, Kristen Quarles, Siobhan Starrs, Hans Sues, Scott L. Wing
Based on exhibition content created by the core team for the David H. Koch Hall of Fossils—Deep Time: Anna K. Behrensmeyer, Kara Blond, Amy Bolton, Matthew T. Carrano, Laura Donnelly-Smith, Elizabeth Jones, Michael Lawrence, Juliana Olsson, Angela Roberts Reeder, Meg Rivers, Siobhan Starrs, Scott L. Wing, Reich+Petch Design International, Richard Lewis Media Group
Specimens prepared and mounted by Research Casting International, NMNH Vertebrate Paleontology Lab, NMNH Paleobiology Collections Management Team
Specimen photography: Smithsonian Institution, with contributions from James Di Loreto, Lucia R. M. Martino, Fred Cochard, Kate D. Sherwood, Chip Clark, Donald E. Hurlbert, John Steiner, Mike Gaudaur, Gary Mulcahey
Illustrations: All by Julius Csotonyi except 4: Peter Sawyer

Published by Smithsonian Books
Director: Carolyn Gleason
Creative director: Jody Billert
Senior editor: Christina Wiginton
Editor: Laura Harger
Editorial assistant: Jaime Schwender
Text: Blake Edgar, based on David H. Koch Hall of Fossils—Deep Time exhibition materials
Book design: Joan Sommers, Glue + Paper Workshop

Title page: The ___ ___ (leaf) and *Secodontosaurus* by a Permian stream.
This page: Flocks of *Pteranodon* (top) and *Icthyornis* fly in a Cretaceous sky.

Image credits (top: *t*; bottom: *b*; left: *l*; right: *r*; center: *c*): 11*tr*: courtesy of the University of Cambridge and the Natural History Museum of Denmark, cast of MGUH 29019; 15*c*: cast of HMV 8246; 21*tl*: with thanks to Iziko Museums of South Africa; 25*tl*: cast of AMNH 2102; *br*: donated by Staatliches Museum für Naturkunde Stuttgart, cast of SMNS 1756; *bl*: model by April Neander, University of Chicago; 27*t*: cast of BSP 1967 I 324; *c*: cast; 33*tl*: courtesy Brigham Young University's Museum of Paleontology, cast of BYU 13019; 41*bl*: cast; *r*: cast; *tc*: cast of HMN 1880/81; *bc*: cast; 47*t*: composite of ROM 1930 and another specimen; *cl*: cast of UALVP 2; 50*c*: cast of FPDM-V6233; *r*: cast of BMRP 2008.4.1; 53*l*: cast of AMNH 6169; 57*b*: cast of PU 18150; 59*t*: cast

Library of Congress Cataloging-in-Publication Data
Names: Edgar, Blake, author. | Johnson, Kirk R. | National Museum of Natural History (U.S.)
Title: Smithsonian dinosaurs and other amazing creatures from deep time / National Museum of Natural History ; Blake Edgar
Description: Washington, DC : Smithsonian Books, [2019] |
Identifiers: LCCN 2018039976 (print) | LCCN 2018041221 (ebook) | ISBN 9781588346629 (eBook) | ISBN 9781588346483 (pbk.)
Subjects: LCSH: Paleontology—Juvenile literature. | Fossils—Juvenile literature. | Dinosaurs—Juvenile literature. | Dinosaurs—Evolution (Biology)—Juvenile literature. | Evolution (Biology)—Juvenile literature
Classification: LCC QE714.5 (ebook) | LCC QE714.5 .E34 2019 (print) | DDC 560—dc23
LC record available at https://lccn.loc.gov/2018039976

Manufactured in China, not at government expense

23 22 21 20 19   5 4 3 2 1